GROUND WORK II
In the Dark

ALSO BY ROBERT DUNCAN

Heavenly City, Earthly City
Medieval Scenes
Poems 1948-49
Song of the Borderguard
Fragments of a Disordered Devotion
Faust Foutu
Caesar's Gate
Letters (poems 1953-56)
Selected Poems
The Opening of the Field
Roots and Branches
Bending the Bow
Ground Work: Before the War
Fictive Certainties

ABOUT ROBERT DUNCAN

Robert Duncan: Scales of the Marvelous
(Edited by Robert J. Bertholf and Ian W. Reid)

Robert Duncan

GROUND WORK II

In the Dark

A New Directions Book

Some of the poems in this collection first appeared in the following magazines: *Bombay Gin, Credences, Hambone, Ironwood, New Directions in Prose and Poetry, New Poetry* (Australia), *Periodics, Sulfur, Temenos, The Southern Review, Wind Bell*.

The following poems were originally published as broadsides: "The Sentinels" (Kent, Ohio: Costmary Press), "Quand le Grand Foyer Descend dans les Eaux" (San Francisco: Interesection), and "In Blood's Domaine" (Tucson: Black Mesa Press).

"Illustrated Lines" was included in Robert Duncan's *A Paris Visit*, published in a limited edition of 130 copies in 1985 by The Grenfell Press, New York.

Manufactured in the United States of America
First published clothbound and as New Directions Paperbook 647 in 1987
Published simultaneously in Canada by Penguin Books Canada Limited

Library of Congress Cataloging-in-Publication Data

Duncan, Robert Edward, 1919–
    Ground work II.

    (New Directions paperbook; 647)
    I. Title.
PS3507.U629G7   1987   811'.54   87-11033
ISBN 0-8112-1042-1 (pbk.: v. 2)
ISBN 0-8112-1041-3 (hard: v. 2)

New Directions Books are published for James Laughlin
by New Directions Publishing Corporation,
80 Eighth Avenue, New York 10011

Contents

AN ALTERNATE LIFE

IN THE SOUTH

Tears will not start here.   The mountain I see
—misty, ascending—weighs in as if it were a cloud,   is not here;
it is louder, though soundless, than the magpie's song.

Dawn did not start here.   The heart I stand
whose need of you   will obey *your* sense of the right and wrong of it
—for, ultimately, there must be in our geometries—
needs many lives —a meeting place thruout.

Am I so darkend   no ray of the sun will venture?
No will   rays out to touch the release waiting?
No hand reaches or would reach to verify,
quickening into its actual earth element   the visual mountain?

                *

I am talking about the beginnings of an age in my body,
light as a mountain   hanging in the air
no one may lift   from me.   In youth
I think now   this fathering shadow   fell forward
from every glance   drawing to ward me   alarms,
        turnings,   alternate engagements,   what compels.

It is a heavy light shining I am speaking of.
Visibly I am moving over to the other side of the picture.
An old man's hand fumbles at the young man's crotch.
An old man's body is about to tremble.   The painter
is almost cruel in his detail to make clear
this shaking.   I am talking of a voice shaking.

I am shaking the rattling gourd of infancy's play.
At the sombre coda of the natural symphony,
what sweet sweeping memorials the violins impart,
more vigorous than ever   the brassy crescendos,

the drumbeat of the heart penetrates all.   O, yes,
Love will at last let go of me.   Let go of me!
I don't want any longer to wait for the thematic release.

Still. .   as if all the sound were gone into me. .
this sound alone,   the rattling gourd of first things,
so faintly sounds,   plaintive and falling away.

                    *

                    Morning flows over me.   The cold
                    washes up against the warmth of me.
                    I stretch my limbs into it.

                    The new age almost fades from my limbs.
                    All my old youth stretches out to fill my flesh.

                    Up.   Up.   The skin is singing!
                    This skin   addresses the day where I am.

                    *

Tho you were only an incident in an alternate life,
and there I was,   as the Lover always is,
swift, leading,   seeking to release the catches of your shirt,
broody, sweet,   tendering the flame of hurt in the healing,

here, in the one life I am leading, I am,
as the Lover always is,   alone before a hand that holds forth
the burning of a heart for me to eat again.

                    For the sake of the Beloved
in this world   the Everlasting instructs.   I crouch
to eat out the bitter heart from that withholding hand again.

                    *

The Mind   —the fucking Mind!   The stars in Its thought
shine forth in abysses, "Night" spaces,
the fucking alone brought us *deep* into.

                    *

2

Circling, circling, circling,   the matter of Love
the Mind knows   has my own particular death in it.
Wary the predator I am   watches to surprise
the moment when   this hunger will yield in me.

Lovely, ever,   this hunting eye's look of you.
In the alternate life I am visiting early Spring again.
Nothing is revised.   I am again without help.

This matter of Love the Mind knows   has
inconsequential ecstasies in its teasing of Time.

Circling, circling,   I can no longer spell the word
the beast I follow might have said to me.

It is not "Death",   not my own particular time of dying.
So many alternate lives have died in me.
I wake this morning searching for the Life I knew,
like a cemetery in the sun searching,
surrounded by yew trees,   bathed in the blaze of light
and the wash of the sky's blue.

                    *

But that is the little graveyard in Soquel
where you and I walkt together years ago,
and that blue of sky is not today's alternative
but what *really* was,   "ours", I had forgotten.

Here where the tears long stored up will not really start,
it is really raining.   It is almost cold.

The cars rushing past the open door
hiss in the gleam of the road beyond.
There is no full blaze of light.   It comes thru the downpour.

                    *

And "I" come forward to gaze into the downpouring glass,
the black crystal in which I find the world
looking for "me".   I hide in my looking.

When we sit down to dinner, I will put the looking-glass away.
I will put away watching for the furtive movement in the flesh
that betrays what I know is hidden there.
      I will give up   this stalking time,
and we will converse of arts and informative reveries.

      *

So I love what is "real".   How awkwardly we name it:
the "actual", the "real", the "authentic" —What Is.

I have come to it as if I could have been "away",
flooded thru by the sorrow of the unlived, the unanswerd,
tho I knew not and had not the courage of asking
      the question that calld for it,
the real I *did* see.   The real so toucht me

      I could not speak before it.

HOMECOMING

Now truly the sexual Eros will have
      left me and gone on his way.
It is a superstition of our time that
      this sexuality is all,   is
lock and key,   the body's
      deepest sleep and waking.

At break of day and at
      midnight's time of play
you are turnd away from me.

      And for Love's sake
I once in mounting raptures of my flesh, in
      singing nerves and mouthing quest,
gatherd up

the ache and spring of Life
into *Love*   however I could
      make it with you,
I now lie in a dark of my own,
      nursing my body's unquiet watch.

   Angel of this tristesse,
   what would you prepare me for?
   Nothing is broken.   He. . you. .
   will still hold my hand and
      sound me where I am.
   The dearness alone lights my eyes I feel.

   Not until the meaning of our
      house so changes me
   would I read thru to what you mean.

Is it Time?   How I attend
the *"now"* of it,   then in every attention
momentous.   It is the impending
I address as messenger.   Under the
sullen weight of an increase in Time
the hour carries, all,   but my body
heavier than the time it occupies,
      would surrender.

               ✴

It would be a marvel I might await
if I were here—in my eighth set of seven years
      completed, my ninth beginning—
brought into a new teaching.

But this news I brought forward with me thru Time
      reaching so into what is ours
I knew in the beginning in myself.   You
did not institute its orders I have come to know.

Lockt in its solitary vise, its appetite,
the carnal body of me climbd upon your spirit
to light   the darkness wanted out of you.   For company?
A flame?   An ember still?   Bright   solitary eyes,
unseeing,   seek their terminals in Night.

And it seems I cradled in this stare.
It was my share you first accepted to be ours
of me, this unwonted need I have so worn
I know no longer if it be truly there.

                    *

This is my first and final place,
        in the outlands of the sun's decline,
                this dark of the sexual moon,
this cold and shadow
        home   in Time.

            And I, ardent and would-be
                artful talker,   of
            wingéd words,   birds or arrows
                sing thru the air,   soar up

                    not for song alone
            this war and this return

                    but for their end in Time.

            *

            "La politique des vieux,"
it came to me to say in this
            first session of talking in French:
"C'est leur vengeance contre la vie."

        —la vengeance de la Vie contre ma vie—

"Et moi,   je suis maintenant
            dans le foyer de cet âge."

For Time has come into a new age.

6

La veille de ma vieillesse
—fitting that this announcement should come
        in language I do not know to speak,
the marches of the day
        inexpert thruout.   The risk of the wrong
words must charge thru.
                        Another
        has always been here,
                keeping this watch,
dry-eyed,   to scrutinize
        what I dare not see as I go,   weigh
                even the thought-to-be-inconsequential
in the outcome,   exact of it
        the very ache and spring from which
                it thought to come

        to this place,   this *home*-ground,

                this place alone.

                        I was always there
. . . *not there.*

SUPPLICATION

        Let me have the grace to speak of this
        for I would mind what happens here.

Tears came   no more than the token   eyes
    gathering in   to mind the heart
    swells to the brim   yet I savor the loss.

So swift the alternate continent drifts from under.
    Unalterably this plane   carries me in its course.

There was no might-have-been,   there is
    only the one thing   this   I go   to ward

keep of my soul-enforcing   —remembering the kiss.

Do I really want the thunder of this hour,
this mouth my mouth seeks,   this tongue

my tongue addresses,   this Word

to come so entirely into the core of Being?

He, not I,   *he* was shaking.   He did not mean
to corner this feeling.   We will never
            advance   to ward each other.

Who am I?   so alien
to the courses of his youth?   in the wrong?

            *

The moment is spectral and I gather it to be
a part I must play in this stage   not my own
yet forever now in this playing   a part of me
drawn into the pattern of a lordly pretension
the coming forth of the body by day is.

So swift the time-flow drifts away from under,
yet how the filament of continued feeling goes out
to touch upon what's lost from view.

How can I see so   the curve of your lips,
the lilt hear of your sounding of English,
      so far from mine,
and catch again in the glance of eyes   a thrill of being
upon the edge of that panic   I wonder.
something here divines me,   finds me out.

The very doubt of living upon which Life
from its initial darings casts itself abroad
I hear rehearse again   its monologue
meant for the communion of all souls   in you.

            *

      Another plane.   Another time returning home.

Another over-view.   What in me

reaches toward you again and yet, in reaching,

recognizes itself in these ranges,

these majesties,   these desolations,

this wilderness,   far below?

    *

Far as the eyes can reach,   the land
        reaches beyond.   The mind
            sees arms of land reaching out to sea.

Far as the sea's reaches, in the dissolve of horizons,
        the mirage of voyage extends
—the imagined discoveries,   the foreign shores,
        the ports of call,   the shipwrecks, unreal islands,
            the being cast adrift,   the drownings—
as if we recalld the nature of the deep
        out of what we were.   O terra firma, terra infirma,

receive me as you will.   Let me
        return,   entirely yours,
            even to the ununderstandable,
the mountainous urgencies,   the eroding tides,
        this continent,   this age,

            let me. .   return me. .

We near the gate and the towers of the city.

This mirage of thronging powers and lives,
        of thoroughfares and those bridges
            glittering in the sun,   everywhere
addresst to the presiding prospect of this bay,
        wherein the resolution of our watch and ward
            be realized,
                    let me return.

O   daily actual life   entirely what I've known,

   companion and familiar to my love,

admit what I am   deep in your thrall.

THE QUOTIDIAN

   There is no way that daily I have not been
          initiate.
          The admission is all.

At last it comes,   rising from the other side
   in me,   the unalterd
resolution,   my affair with the beginnings of this world
       held to the last
governor of an ever-returning coda,   the daily rituals:

the unfolding, the stretching, the turning upon the spine,
   surfacing,   breathing in the day's air,
   conscious,   opening eyes to steal
a look entirely mine of you
   —delicious, how
         ever close it is to first seeing,
the feeling of this awakening,

this stealing of a life-fire,   of this
   Promethean infancy,
from the foundries of a parental embrace,
   up from the debris of dreams
        into the body desire prepared
to rise again from its own ashes—

   familiar,   strange,   familiar,
just here,   this joyous quietude,

already troubled by the falling away
　　of remnants of another life
　　　　　into Lethe.

　　　*

I do not speak here of that river
　　you read to be an allusion
　　　　　to ancient myth and poetry,
though it too belongs to a story,
but of a rushing underground in the very life-flow,
　　a sinking-back,
　　　　　a loss of the essential in the
shadows and undertow—

　　from which I come up into the day time.

The bedside radio I turnd on just as I woke
　　announces the minute of the hour.

　　　　In the realm of this mind I return to,
the steps of the sun have already
　　set into motion and number
　　　　　the rememberd measures.

Seven o'clock in the morning renews itself over breakfast
　—the richness of coffee, the full flavor of the bread
toasted, the assorted jams and marmalades— we
　　　　　initiate the naming of the day
with the institution of a choice of　things
　　and repetitions of our way,　yet
altering minutely the course of decisions　thruout

　　　　design　and unalterable variations.

　　　*

I speak here of riding the earth
round into the sunlight again,
of this "It came to pass that . . . "
in which we take place,　ours,　swift,
inevitable, answering,　this current

11

turning upon the axis of another year,
this ever   growing older in turning

      into Spring again,
coming into Easter,   into the
     passions of resurrection,   the commingling
of life-streams in this ceremony of pouring,
      into the precession of equinoxes in the Great Year
        to the flowering insurrections of Aquarius.

    *

One more week and it will be here
    still
         "It",   the persistence I seem to
draw this "I" from.   The one
    fountain, Memory —the other,
        Lethe, the Healer.   The two waters
pour forth from the mouth of It.   The wars,
    the rage for the retribution of wrongs,
       the Easter Man upon his cross,
the successions of loss and love
    found anew,   the stroke,
       the demolition of all goods,
the contest with evil,
    the communal joy— pass on.

        They were what we volunteerd,
   incidents the mind barely recalls.
             Let me then
    recite the seasons as I would recite
       the passing of anarchists and great kings.

    Lovely now
       news comes from the South,
gifts from another time I
    most hold in losing.   Did I really
take place there?

In that history too?

Down under the seasons I know?

*

It goes as it will.
Its haunt is an edifice of air
most sound in what we do not hear   but draw
from out of whose invisibilities
illustrious hints of visage where
our human faces come to light,   a music
our music might steal away from.   I'd make
my way   in strains of song   to you
as ever.   Let the aweful rivers
come through into the one bed,
the momentary coursing.

Take your time with me.
I belong to it.

Daily the minutes pass.   The hours
return into themselves.   The first time seems
already worn.   The wear
yields to transformations of the air,
I long for its verging upon meaning so.

Unbearable,   the pathos into
    beauty of this theme,

the changes,   the constancy.

*

Every day I am away,   I remember.
The night of each day lapses into a deepening of gold.
Everyday gods of the ordinary preside even in dreams and hold
the keys of the locks from which this language flows.

Every day these household conduits and currents,   these
    circulations of water and of fire.
Every day the shadow of this mountain grows in the mind.

Every day, in the alembic of an increasing time come due,
   glows and quickens into an instant flare to ash
   this mountainous desire
and prolongs youth's passionate realities—bright spectral residue—
into this dim reminder in which Life aches to die
   and, lasting, watches every day pass by.

        *

In youth   what did I know?
The violence of a fierce weather shook me so
I could not move for it   or rusht abroad
as if my soul were all fire and rain mixt in a cloud.

Love I would not have allowd
alone could release the soul of what I was to be
I sought in the flaming up of sexuality
yet, raging in the beauty of the flower,
tore at the heart before the fruit to be devourd devourd
   what was.

Here, in the foyer of my age,
the passing of the storm remains upon the page
where I reread myself   and all
that once befell comes once again to fall.
It is a text of after-images.

There was a rumor of me I almost overheard
I now construct from word to word
a song that in the alternate life I pourd
forth upon the radiant air that my world with me be stirrd.

Man's a bird of omen, dark as anthracite, upon that golden bough,
and all his words, the rapturous reiteration of some vow,
an animal call in anguish, a summoning of fate,
in which the strife,   the wearing and the after-glow
of what was realized,   the total thrust of a life,

charges the contour of a momentary line
as if throughout we meant but to sign   this place and time.

        *

Every day that I am here   I recall
early notes in the sounding of the late.

What we have shared, our life in me,
the leavings and returnings of these years,
withdrawn from what bright multiplicities
prepared
                              Love
that overtakes me and pervades the falling of the light

        touches upon a presence that is all.

❖❖❖❖❖❖❖❖❖❖❖❖❖❖

TO MASTER BAUDELAIRE

TOWARD HIS MALAISE

When I come to Death's customs,
    to the surrender of my nativities,
that office of the dark too I picture
    as if there were a crossing over,
a going thru a door,   in obliteration
—at last, my destination Time will not undo—

    and leave taking, good bye
to the calendars of our old friendship,
    its green shade and its scatterd
distributions of the light,
    vernal leaves and autumnal leavings,
seasonal variations of day and night,
    referring to you thruout.

I love the trunk of our human tree
    we grow from   and yet gratefully
will let go,   let the wind
    tear me away.   It's an old romance,
this ode to winter again
    and to every intensity of who I am
swept on into the drifts of this
    animal debris and decay of intensities.

O, in the green of your first reading,
    as, here, writing, the stem—
the sentence ex-pressing itself
    the flow of life into its leaf-work
in the greater life the sun promises,
    the free-going, the fluid passages,
the answerings,   the soul
    enfolding in soul,   the full

summer's work and the sharp
    first hints of color fall advances—

it is as if the youthful green
    that drew us as lovers together
were no more than a gathering
    sheath, a knot of meaning
the reader was eager to find,
    a door the mind forced open for itself,
for this outburst in sere and cold,
    this gold and crimson finale.

I know thru and thru the brutal
    facts in which this unity
        —grand illusion of what is lovely—
takes hold. What I know
    makes fierce indeed the drive
        of my striving here. Hatreds
as well as loves flowd thru as the
    sap of me.   And we too,
        my life companion and I,
entertaind our projects and fancies,
    playd house and kept company
upon the edge of what we never knew then
    you made clear was there
        in the human condition—your *Ennui*

    plus laid, plus méchant, plus immonde,

that we would never have come to,   yet
    in the depths of Poetry
I have so long ever gone to and ever
    returnd myself from,   beyond
the furies' nest, the squalor of these
    back streets, ravaged fields,
and the grinding, the drains,
    the sullen aftermaths of wars and
man's industrious sexuality,   there is a nursery
    deepest of all you knew

and pourd into our common stream
　　　this residue of an Eternal Admission,
whose nurse, formidable Muse of Man's Stupidities
　　　—we are surrounded by her evidence—
counts out into hours　the endlessness
　　　of a relentless distaste.

AMONG HIS WORDS

　　　Animated the Baudelairean leavings fill.　The chamber with a rich perfume comes in.　Shuts the door.　Enclosing.　This immensity, these shadowy profundities.　Giddy extensions into green.　Vertigo.　Draw the blind then.　Leave sight out.　Draw the line to illuminate the wall behind seeing.　Dangle the lights.　Throw out the century.　The shouts from the street will still come in.　The air will still be heavy.　Here.　Running out over the heapt sheets and bed clothes, the worn comforters Time allows, the aging meat of belly and thighs, the vital flaccidities.

　　　Runnels of soild sound.　Consonance in a confusion of vowels sounding a grave determination.　The chamber of sleep swells, smokes, stiffens into clouds of yellow with the urgency against the howl interior to our dismay that a continued charge in the word demands.

　　　Tainted hands.　From a faint aroma.　Barely.　Overwhelms in　its.　Vastness.　Voluptuous.　Desolation.　The Baudelairean words.

THE FACE

Be still, whatever deep onward current flowing, steady
your face entirely receptive, my soul, to mirror this presence
needs, as if in the eternal holding of a breath, to sound your depth
needs hear　this dark glassy clear surface waiting upon

reflections.   It is time to reflect,   to let the feeling come forward
from the foundations of the pouring waters of a face so steady
as if sleep tranquil and gleaming had ever a ready place,
a letting go of striving, protesting, knowing, grasping.

Not to know, not to receive, not to come and go all rippling surfaces,
but, welling up from the beginning, a vacuity, an utter *surface*
surfaces, and, for the solemnity of the moment, I feel
clouds, drift, the sky, the trees, moving in the wind out there, all

but invisibly moving in their own life in me, the shadow of an other face
looking into me, that face returning, radiant, addresst, that smile
those deep looking eyes, lovely thruout   the mystery of person
centering and holding at attention   this world,

this great moving image, just now beginning again to be
troubled, yet, as if Eternity had a hold there, at last
lasting, and I in that hold held,   I, held here, to the last,
in your searching yourself in me,   in my reflecting.

                    *

AT CAMBRIDGE AN ADDRESS TO YOUNG POETS NATIVE TO
THE LAND OF MY MOTHERTONGUE

From the language I do not know to speak the voice not mine to speak speaks to me. The feel draws my feeling of speaking above into the realm of these words in the dark of my own hearing luminous so that there is a shining realm above invaded by numbers and ratios of a mind in which all that I am most to mind trembles to begin. *Neiger.* I almost understand what it says. The soft neigh of a horse white and falling everywhere else into still another world into whose stillness no sound of footfall echoes but here there is a residue of hooves. *"Les fils qui nous remuent"* invisibles —a line of Baudelaire leaks through— lead me to believe. Soundings and listenings enthrall my belief and steal it away. Bereft, I am still listening. As I had only to believe then, murmuring, babbling, whining, howling, shattering the divine columns of language surrounding me long ago—yesterday— but a second ago while-where I lay in the house of men and women sounding. I was a serpent. The seed of a mind to come coild before language and recoild in the waves of talking around me.

Now as then I lose myself in words above my head, in following words naked of meaning, as I was in the beginning, hearing the magic voice beyond my sight, out of sight, puts on and removes faces not meant for me.

They are mouthing each other in the passages between words and I hear the sound of sucking, the holding of breath and the releasing of breath in vowels I will yet come to from—the labials, the nasals, the fricatives. I will yet come to. Behind the mouth an intent to speak to me returns again and again to the same patterns and urgencies. The same hooves the tread of feet moving through sentences in phrases, the verges of time, of march and mazurka. It is 1921, remember. Someone has let loose the tango. The seed of the mind to be is in a lull a bye bye that comes round to say good bye again.

This is not my first year. I am in my third. Say it is the beginning of May, in 1921, my third year, and I am in a trouble with talking in my fatherland in my mother-tongue. I walk in my sleep a form of talking. I talk in my sleep where my feet are moving toward my not talking. It is a time of forever asking, forever trying being, forever seeking, of this dying to know even as I go away from knowing.

Had I an unbounded infancy before I sought the bond words promised me? In the thought of that year I am bound again for this place where I come across my loss of boundaries I know nothing of. Yet. In my fifty-ninth year I have still a root that draws deep from the vanisht world above in order to sound itself. You think this is a history or yet gets not to be only a history.   Did Bruno of Nola walk these streets and Marlowe in his ruddy youth run with these boys?   What do they mean to do?   Not here, not now.   At the touch of What Is, Time undoes its holds.   The giantesses of 1921 in their frocks of emerald crêpe de chine and cloth of gold have long passed into the glare of that shadow as far from what you know as William Shakespeare's sweet lips and his phantom lover.   England and America pass each other from under us into that glare.   And you who are young for the moment see me as I would cast the spell of my name one alone and yet entirely given over to the many movements beyond saying the man I am no more alone than that, the glowing intent of the word so overtaking me I waver and go out, in the language I know no more than a dark shadow, the threshold of another language as it were Heaven, as in the beginning beyond me, above me, entirely promising me to me, the New World, before me, drawing me.

LE SONNET où sonne la sonnette
dès dernières jours toujours
fait son retour

each day I secure the meaning
of my name in yours

in you   my drift

and the shores

in you   derived

in what is ours

the boat and the oars

the sail before the ongoing
winds

the river
wider than the horizon of
our lives

*

—we make our "Owl and
Pussy Cat"   séjour

and once again   revive

bright infancies

that take their stand

angelic warriors to surround

the troubled heart
in what is otherwise

monstrous sense and sound

    transformd

transfounded in this fond

    nonsense and unsound

    confidence—

a little music of a mandoline,
    a little charm,
a little iambic incantation

to welcome in the night
    to sing a song
of six pence and our
    mere lives
our little histories in one

    amidst

this watery waste and its
    horizons

upon we know not whether
    an approaching storm
or deadly calm

    revelation of real weather

we belong to

    each other

serenade

across the fearful flood there
    comes

the strumming of a toy guitar
(it was a mandoline;   it was
       a small bán-jó   máde
dimly real in its own moonlight)
the who-hooting of an owlish
       lover who would delite
the purring answer of a
       fond response

—figures fantasy would recall
playd upon the strings
       of what is real

even as the scene, the moment

       begins   to fade

the refrain remains,

le sonnet d'amour

       où sonne la sonnette
dès dernières jours toujours

       fait son retour.

POUR SOUFFRIR L'ENVIE JUSQU'À L'AMOUR EN VIE
LE NON-RIRE   IL FAUT QU'IL RIE

Au seuil du soleil   noir

soleil   clair

le nom   change,

l'unité   (se) dérange

la douleur   le deuil

d'ailleurs

die Sonne

recommence à faire   là

limitation de la lumière,

les dix zones des astres d'or

avancent

l'imitation de la chaire

solaire

dans l'accident psycho-chimique

de la chair.

❖❖❖❖❖❖❖❖❖❖❖❖❖❖

SETS OF SYLLABLES, SETS OF WORDS,
SETS OF LINES, SETS OF POEMS ADDRESSING:
VEIL, TURBINE, CORD, & BIRD

PRELIMINARY EXERCISE:

What does a turbine veil?   a bird avail what chord?
I heard a bird whir no word, felt
a turbine shadow turning from the floods of time
electric currents the darkness stirrd,
and trees in blaze of light arose
casting shadows of speech, seductive, musical, abroad.
It was a single tree.   It was a word of many trees
       that filld the vale.
It was a store of the unspoken in the bird
that whirrd the air, that every occasion of the word
      overawed.

NOTES DURING A LECTURE ON MATHEMATICS:

And now I know it.   The irrational is trying.
Prove it as permissible speech.
SET talk.   No one has it.   We are going into it.
IT received a name.   Name it.
We are in the mystery of the name.
Sets are: collections, a thing, a team, a jury, an
  army,   made up out of   —a set of lines—
  sufficiently precise, assuming,
  absolving, solution, solve
  purely operational
  . . . .
  figure and language   predicting.

THE RECALL OF THE STAR *MIRAFLOR*

1

The turban and the veil
lead us to the turbine in the vale

2

where we have been before
flowers forever bloom—it is the dale of profusions,
of the mind's lingering, of the heart's stop,
here, where perfumes and colors pour,
here, where the magic top spins,

3

Miraflor

4

is the name of the place we were
—you and I are—   in this music
for *Ever*?

5

For I come ever to you here there.
Now the intoning of the color/sound *hwyll*,
Now the returning mandala deepens,
Savors and odors recall this star.

THE NAMING OF THE TIME *EVER*

FIRST: SONG TWO

Morning-bird, whose song our lives,
calling forth in five notes
beauty entire within this horizon,

SECOND: SONG FIVE

Guru,

THIRD: SONG ONE

sweet Western Song-sparrow,
awakening each day
beyond in us,
valiant ego singer
recall me there.

FOURTH: SONG THREE

Miraflor is thy song
to us ever venturing
tones we hear belong
chords in color ring,

FIFTH: SONG FOUR

bell   horizons
tonguing   air.

I POUR FORTH MY LIFE FROM THIS BOUGH

This veil of flowering now
weaves itself before tomorrow morning
cords potential of our returning
ring beyond ring,   horizon calls
transfiguring each point,   far footfalls,
so that the transmission is
all of echoes, and bliss,
ecstatic leap thruout toward trembling,
leads deep into this thing,
Miraflor, star-nest of every bird,
bright message in which word
upon word dances and transpires

and sound shadows and fires
of color releases into sound.

In this mirage I found
each return, self and soul
pour forth into the bowl
space and time all emptiness
holds forth, and here rest
as in a mirror's face
ever still this pouring grace.

I pour forth my life
ever light star magic bird
being cord veil and turbine,
transmitter of retractions and emissions
in the course of things
recoursing, sounding changes, things resounding,

so that the source has changed in me
and what was bound to be is free
—so said the bird upon the tree who was no more
than a figure workt in the leafy patterning of the veil
and from the embroidery of a bough
into the veilings and unveilings of that work
long pourd forth his soul in song.

THE TURBINE

For I your boy of brass bright star the force
song turns of wheel in heart man strength streams fire
weave still the veil and spell from word to chord
green course from spring to fall I take my source
where sun down dark the earth goes round to tire
and seek dear night my myrrh and red bird pour
in turn from light to dim and dim to sleep.

Let mind and self go out, let breath to breath
go back, let yet what throne, what name, what deep
spin hwyll and crown of me go fast to death

in love's sweet care I would not part from here
but day to day for you stay where you are
all truth takes heart in whom I've come to hear
bell tones and scents this star call forth once more.

WHAT THE SONNET MEANS THE SONNET MEANS:

Tho the turbine hum with power and the source of enlightenment would crown the spirit, I would leave my spirit, if it so chose, to their play and go still on my way; and, if my soul craved the currents of Buddha compassion, give up my soul-suffering to whatever washing away from being it seek, for I go swiftly and even alone to what I love.   I follow the Way of Romance, a mere story of loving and the household we found in the design of the veil.   I am entirely a creature of the veil, there my life cord, there my bird song of scents and colors.   I go gladly on into stages of pain, of aging, of loss, of death, that belong to the passionate, and, if the wheel so return me, I shall embrace again birth cord and pang of this animal being and come into whatever desires and delusions in memory of you and this passing time in your care.

Now She Who Will One Day Recall Me writes:

No initiation, you are right, dear boy,
  Just the simple facts of life
      including death
      rocks   goats   and herbs.

For *this* ever am I Love's good beast and dancer,
Sundown's herald, Dawn's answerer,
      Night's companion in Day's realm.

FOR THE ASSIGNMENT OF THE SPIRIT

the secret of a smile

has passt into the mind-store
    into time and mind-change.

Into the center of what we mind
    this in-formation
    we return to see
in the inward gaze,   the
    rising into the mouth
    of this secret

reserve   returnd
    and mindful;

has passt into the hand-work
    the eye has rejoiced in this smile
has passt this way
    this working of the wood went,

the hidden fire within
    rising thruout into a smiling,
    a sealing in the surface
    interworking of the tree's life
    and another
mind-life   so that we see
    the wood   and we see
the willing of the image
    brought out   in it,

so that the image perfects itself in our
    seeing and we would not
let it go   from us.   The art!
    the art we address

has passt into the mind-store,
    into the realm of our musing,
into our adoring.   Sealing, the smile
    rests   before us

and the mind would entirely
       go over to this state,
this image   of an Eternal Mind

more true to us   now it seems
       this Eternal Presence
than the passages, the changes,
       the burning thru and over   Life is
in us,   our living
       in using our stuff up

has passt into the alembic,
       into the workings of air,
the devouring,   into the work
       of wet and flood, the rotting
and tearing away, into the fire,
       the charring, the eroding, the earth
elements

work now the secret of what the
       smile   is,
the presence of the fire's work

the wearing away in the smile

       that seal too   there

       the mind

taking in   deep

       the burn.

THE CHERUBIM (I)

*

Across the ark   the wings
commingling
touch in touch   until
the will
of each other both close
            dark
and dreaming eyes,
        lion-visaged
man-gazed rapacious bird-
        bright   fire   cloud

rustling.   What we see
    was only a moment's
shadow   yet full

        and animal.

            What we heard . . .
what we felt . . .   was that
        spell binding
promise   before us,
        leading,   yet now,
after us,   pursuing.

For it is of the stalking I am speaking,
of the tread sinister that follows us thru time,
the attendant wings
surrounding the voice I fear we
        being to hear

            and you. . . .

        *

In everything humane,
but in this moment   coverd,

wingd time over them
hovering, hushing, hesitating,

two halves of the one world
about to close   before the return
—before the touch— their approaching

     fearfully

     waiting,

       *

reach beyond themselves   and here
    just where each
   wing but touches each

    rime appears.

THE CHERUBIM (II)

Pourquoi   la vie   a-t-elle crée   —s'est-elle crée—
une bouche dedans laquelle elle a secreté   cette langue?
Pour bavarder   pour parler   pour dire . . .?

Pourquoi cette langue fleurissait-elle de cette   gorge,
cette gueule qui a toujours quel désir,   quelle
envie d'avaler tout,   de retourner tout à la vie
d'où elle était née?

*

In their roaring   extend   featherd wing
to feathered wing   the lion-   wind in its cloud
            towers
at the center of all horizons   and waits
            time's
falling into itself   this roar announces.

*

Eyes meeting eyes so touch
            we fall
into time out of time, space out of space,   your face
ever comes forward to meet me where I am   we are.

How quiet the house in this   unquieting arrest
                  still
you have made room for me   here
            in the opening of a door   you have made a place
of rest in which I am   only I   only you
            life   declaring itself in us.

*

Why has She, Life, created . . .   what has She   created. .
                    a mouth?
in which She has secreted this tongue.

            To babble, to talk, to speak, to say
                        . . . what?   and why,
does this tongue flower forth in this throat,
          this gullet   that always desires so,
has such a need,   to swallow and to return
          everything   to Her, to Life,
from which She was born?

STYX

And a tenth part of Okeanos is given to dark night
    a tithe of the pure water   under   earth
so that the clear fountains pour from rock face,
    tears stream from the caverns and clefts,
    down-running, carving woundrous ways in basalt resistance,
    cutting deep as they go into layers of time-layerd
        Gaia where She sleeps—

the cold water, the black rushing gleam, the
    moving down-rush, wash, gush out over
    bed-rock, toiling the boulders in flood,
    purling in deeps, broad flashing in falls—

And a tenth part of bright clear Okeanos
    his circulations— mists, rains, sheets, sheathes—
    lies in poisonous depths, the black water.

Styx   this carver of caverns beneath us is.
Styx   this black water,   this down-pouring.

The well is deep.   From its stillness
    the words our voices speak   echo.
    Resonance follows resonance.
    Waves of this sounding come up to us.

    We draw the black water, pure and cold.
    The light of day is not as bright
    as this crystal flowing.

Three thousand years we have recited its virtue
    out of Hesiod.
                Is it twenty-five thousand
since the ice withdrew from the lands   and we
came forth from the realm of caverns where
the river beneath the earth   we knew
    we go back to.

Styx pouring down in the spring from its glacial remove,
from the black ice.

Fifty million years—from the beginning of what we are—
we knew the depth of this well to be.

Fifty million years deep   —but our knowing deepens
        —time deepens—
                              this still water

we thirst for   in dreams we dread.

THE SENTINELS

Earth owls in ancient burrows clumpt
the dream presents.   I could return to look.
No other fragment remains.   I wanted owls
and brought them back.   The grey-brown earth-
haunted grass and bush and bushy birds
so near to death, silent as a family photograph,
still as if the sound of a rattle were missing,
the owls shifting into the stillness, thicket and hole
alive, impassive witnesses thrive there
as ever—I've but to close my eyes and go.
The rest of that field and the company
I was among in that place are lost—ghost folk,
passing among whom I was a wraith,
awake, studious, writing, the blur
marrd and almost erased,   unmarkt events.
It was night and cold and the light there
was an after-light.   I wrapt my naked body
in my comforter against that wind.   I
do not—I can not—I will not, trying,
recite the rest.   It was grey day in an absence of the sun.
It was a place without a rattling sound,
a deaf waiting room this place is close upon.
The scratching of my pen and my bending thought
move from this margin and return.   Morning shrinks.
The owls shiver down into the secrets of an earth
I began to see when I lookt into the hole I feard
and then saw others in the clump of grass.
I was dreaming and where I dreamt a light had gone out
and in that light they blind their sight and sit
sentinel upon the brooding of owl-thought, counselings
I remember ever mute and alive, hidden in all things.

AN EROS/AMOR/LOVE CYCLE

1

My nose was not there, I did not smell the air,
the hair,   I did not see.   I did not taste.
I did not light the lamp,   every thing was your embrace
and almost dying there,   O every thing
was in the passing away into the kiss
dark kindling and stark deep looking into the dark
rapture I knew your avid answering face
was there.   And I,   I was all its care.

O, to be in your care!   You   ring for me.
Your eyes so took my eyes into their stare I could not see.

The man-bird pierced by sight
floods out disburst until the furthest reaches of the night,
comes into an immense fluttering
and all the rest of me in need embodying comes to
an   other   triumphant   beating   wing.

2   [Song: circa 1933]

Love sick,   his eyes have stricken mine.
Mu-zick,   I've just begun to pine.
Let me go on along this line as far as it goes.
The smitten worm   swooning   works away at the heart of the rose
and everywhere   a rich perfume
          grows . . .

They tell me that poetry if it were truly   what it is
should have nothing to do with rime   or this
sweet agony of loving you, they say that words
properly dont flow from me or reach towards those   I love
and yet my heart beats   in every phrase as if
you toucht me there as I sang   I sing again . . .

Love sick, the look of you is on my mind.
Mu-zick,   I wont let it go and so I find

3   STRUCTURE OF RIME

each time . beloved Master of Rime . your name . comes
. round . and you descend the ladders of . sound . by sound
. bells . entwine the districts of our town . my mind . I mind
. how in every return your command has grown .
and . again . my nature has come home in yours . and flown
. beyond . where all the world of thought is light and blond .

yet night is everywhere and I await a dark of meaning there
. your face . how deep your gaze I see . grace .
          opens a well I thought a ladder in me .
and echoing . ascending in the descent or descending to ascend .
  your feet . sound time in me
. bells ring in other worlds I cannot see .
I see . imprint in sound . sound in the imprint . where you have been
. enduring .
where you have yet to be.
By the fountain well of ancient waters I attend .
the evening bells announce . their measures . your footfall, footstep
. by step measures .
time . across the opening distances . measures .
          extend and return . this telling
. recall of my nature in what I am.   Rime
sweet   deepening   eternal   incidental
O   the sweet deepening eternal incidents of me
     you know!

4

This foyer—this language—burns within language,
     this light aflame in the light,
     this darkening in the realms of the dark,
     my breath in his breathing . . .

5

Let the Sun come into my mind to stand a part.
In the subterranean chambers where the water ran
from stone-ledge wept, gleam, shadow-radiant shine   this art

Phallus, erect, silent, compels   I, wet,
bent down and took into my throat the sign,
here alone my horizon spells its palace, head,
     live station and arrest.   How long,

sweet festival,   I mouth the opening of the song,
the only presentation of the hidden solar   one   in you
     the pulse   the rod   the a-waiting time

all requires   signal load-stone of apprehensions   spires
the heart grows tall and reaches   comes to head in me
and, candling, quick enthralls and leaping
fires.

"Dante's Inferno" the knowing calld this place,
somewhere   the Île de France   1956   this
dim arena in time. .   In Sodom   was there such a hall?

where Osiris of the Egyptians, Lord and Solitude of Flesh, yet stands,
and mind goes over to address its thriving there.
Let the moon take back its rays and I'll return this light.

When it was done I slept   and sleeping still
this fountain   this stiffening music   this sun sprung live
and alert within   all shadow   all stalk   I stalk

amanita-power-plant bird-up   from its nest of hair
wet in me the magic tower fills full with seed
and all is anointed in dreaming will.

6   The Epigraph in sequence from Rumi, *Divan-e Kabir*

I read the stories of lovers night and day.
Now I have become a story in my love for you.

                puis sommes descendus au vaisseau
                    avons posé la quille aux brisants
                            là-bas
où la mer cherchait toujours
                des marges nouvelles
                        des envahissements
                            des confusions éternelles
la démarrons!   la faisons
            le passage
                                    au-delà
        dérivés

                        did not want to
                            drift
        I said yet   this is my drift
dérêvés   O   outside my own dream
            having no tongue of my own,
                    no mouth
dreamd here   there
                        le rêve
            —ses marées,   sa parole où nos paroles se noient
            Quoi? Quoi? Quoi?   birdcry and wave roar
    "to see and perceive things *here*"   to hear   in this hearing   what sounds
depth appears   unfathomable   obscure   foundations
                    ses courants du fond

A partir du cinquième chant   Οδυσσέως Πλάνη

     l'errement d'Ulysse   courants de ma soixantaine

L'île . . . a-t-elle réellement existé?   N'est-elle au contraire

    tide wash and undertow   qu'une fiction poétique   sea

castings abroad   au gré de l'imagination et des contes populaires?

    old stories   spectral heroes   the air

of an ancient magic before history Orpheus cast before *us*   lost

    but where the song was   an island

    on doit pouvoir la localiser   et la reconnaître

    the Cave   the Birds   the Sources   the Trees

ancestral leavings   seek   first of all

    the Springs   in these passages   back of Pound's cantos

    my keys.

        The Moon is full

whose sheath of reflections flows out over the shining strand below us

   ici   franchissons ces parages

    the silken light   the silver fountain therein

    the dark metal

mobiles,   obscurs,   capricieux,   changeants . . .

IN WONDER   [Passages]

Beryllisticus, hic,   in Lamina Chrystallina   pending

will see   all things

earth bares and flood   carries with it

coursing

and in carbuncle or ruby stone

explore

"We are alone in taking something else into account."

To stir   these
latencies

writing—*"norgol"*   enters in.   Different languages.

What language?   I heard to write down.

Versions.   What version of my life is this in front of me?

"a house with a boat on its roof"

"a single letter of the alphabet"   "*A*" then, a note to Z   I would

remember

"the figure of a running man whose head has been conjured away"

The rebus has been removed from its language into what we feard it was.

Shall we learn the German
germane to the reading of the Sphinx?

She refuses to speak.

Back of the genital throne   the sphincter awakens and moves the dream.

Hinter den German ein Traumen-Figures liegt avec des Engeln kasts

speech-shadows   upon the waters

the ear-hear-eins für   Images into sounds come

Ur tterances   back to us

trans missions

memorize the sphinxter   bud-thought   disclosure   works

sweet eye

a smell of courses rose

dressing and undressing to spread this news   this well

that slumbers

seeing.   Terrorances.

FOR MICHAEL PALMER   who *alzo*   may   work   alone

spracht   our Dee   no language

this writing as such   its intercourses

parmi des faux amis   ses erreciónes

means

Ists gut?

Chaque à son goût exquis arrive à la *SAVEUR*

que la langue désire

the inner-ear-temple altar nexus of our Hearing
                                        Equilibrations
                                        Accelerations and

diminuendos

translator   host   draw-cord

(the poem contracts   to be   what it is

yet to be   condensate

And did I not tell you clearly the first angel appears here

      guarding against this   utterance

(I could not say   I dared not

      write   a word   I

                  "Nor-gol"—a name?   Out of what

science fiction

      IT   The Strangler   showing   his/her   omens

        the line   or rope,   the divining weights

     How powerfully thy footsteps pass all boundaries!

     The writing on this wall   surpasses languages.

Hast thou a taste for rime?   dim soundings of Memory's
      bright shoals in Night's neglected waters   Time
                      resonant?

     Benevolentiam vobis excitavére

        the Beryl   a green sea   enclosure

              et conciliavére   sempiternam

                 holds up for Ever

a light   the Verdant Mind   having such a Heavy Presence

     Vestrae admirande Virtutes   EXCELLENTISSIMAE MAIESTATI

       Miranda/Mirandus   up tight about

the right word   ghostly balance   What to contain so?

       attends.

CONSTRUCTING THE COURSE OF A RIVER IN THE PYRENEES

(For G.M.P. by Grtde Stein)

The city I dreamt about was not O.
I was not among the weepers at Puivert.
I was not among the quite ones.

Yet the door was open,
Time passt
and the light was queer I saw.

This is the way over the water
where I am arrested in the lady's presence
descends into the changes of the quest.

What remains counts to two only.
Steps surrounding the central postscript,
a hand's breadth from the quick the watch stops.

No, I didnt dream about that city, no
place had been mine there and peace
rules the quarter this rain comes from.

The rest is the wind's, and the wind is old.
We two rest at last in the wind's path.
We too set up our tents in the wind's quarantine.

Again we are left when the fair is over.
Again, owlet, we have misst the queen's play.
Again, after all is done, we will not place or be passt over.

And there was a war around us.

IN WAKING

the life there was   is.
That's the fact we celebrate in passing.
        The loss
is not recent but
    known in the beginning   so that
waking in the dark I grasp my skull,
    hands finding out   the feel of it,
the lines coming thru as I find myself
    speaking, mouthing them, *"We . . ."*
—toes *(mes orteils)*, naming,   flexing,
    the calves of my legs *(mes mollets)* heavy—
I am remembering.
          What it meant
it means   a round   from other lives
    for rime.

They are members of a divine company
in this world   the other world attending
    Mind   our   *speculum*
        ". . . wake together."
Their sight in us   opens   morning's vistas
    our *via imaginativa*   day's eyes.
The way Life opts   we follow thru,
    I   in your company   *seeing*   name.
In the customs of speech I have long known
    —native to what speech?—

a few words from an other language

      I am seeking

come thru   you again   where

    foreign to myself   I am

reminded   yours   in every light.

      *

    Whose lions in this stage   scent already

our faltering steps   and will prey

    upon the body's marches

opening gates in night's dream enclosures

    to the disclosures of a last day

following in the wake of a time that was ours,

    years in whose count we have thrived

rip from the feast in what we are

    a further wake of what we were.

And so I come to speak of pain again.

    How are you this morning?   I try out

the faint ache of coming to,   then lose all,

    loosening the strain in my study of you,

drawing your sleeping face   to divine

      my truth and hold

from which I move   at times like this.

      *

I saw the borderguard.   I saw the sleeping lion.

      Wherein I saw   fused

from dream, from reading, from what I had taken

    out of that painting by Rousseau direct it seemd

      yet "given"   for the sight came "back" to me from an horizon

I knew by heart   I had always   known

      the lion had left his pride.

     In which the guardian's dream deepens

into watch,   the moon

      over all restored,

and in that place takes hold

     in time.

They are the members of a wake behind speech,

    song   our echoing.

And now from Rumi

the lion of the Lord in Love

delivers himself up from his hunger.

He lays himself down in the nets of creation to find his release.

And who am I?   the man sleeping at the border asks,

that in my love dream sleep I have become

    the guardian of the lion?

FROM THE FALL OF 1950
DECEMBER 1980

Bliss! I am extinguisht in thee   my
blessing that yet in this "I" to see
la blessure that in this world leads me to this
as if in return.

          *

This color bleeds thru from the rose dorée
rose d'aurore
and yet I may, because of you, delay the while
to reminisce   of my

"thou" that, though dismisst from our common speech,
comes thru when I saw "you"   today   dawn
speakest secreted underlying pulse,
roarest fierce in the sweet syllable.

          *

Even in jest your name
tenders affection's first flamey seedling
echo to awake the life in my life
animal delite has come to whose call

and all jokey and yet deep going
I come always from the edge of sorrow
to seek the shore of your regard
enduring   let day after day

fall from us into place   they
come again to rime.   In thirty years
happy chance of a refrain yet renders
desire more exquisite

as if searching the tone again and again
where pang and rest
in one arrest combine and change
until I do not know

—the moment costs so dear—
if sight or sound grows near
and upon a wave of coloring brings forth
 this key

or, haunting these resonances of a word,
touches me, intensifies,
minds me, guides my thought

—in transports of what I see and hear
"we" are ever present,
bright ghosts most lightening the
shade they love—
      unlocks
the dark to come forth from day
and sparks in night
one glowing star to shine.

   *

To shine! From the Fall of 1950
now December 1980 my soul
with yours "thine" as if one freshet
forth from the cleaving of the rock, my mind

arising there ever in the searching regard
you initiate where I my dwelling
make near in farthest reaches
seeks to flame light won

in the lightest tone wind-flower
pale gold against the white, and blue
sky upon those edges burns more blue
—the line would lose itself in color!

Let my verse be high and dry until
your mind flows in its own waters.
Let my rimes flow then into a rivering
until the feeling fires I mean

the whole to shine!   It is a song of praise
in which the wound into its river runs
and winding shines from time to time,
dark and daylight glimmering

with hints of an ever happening rime.

It is a painting of the ephemeral
where what we took to be water glares
and in the heart of a solar mirror flares.

A memorial ode for the first decade of New College—that deeper purposes be remembered in present action.   In the working of the lines I keep the presence of tens to count: ten lines in each of the two decads; counts of ten—syllables or words—in each line; with sets of embedded tens in which words and syllables cooperate.   Thus the proposition of energies directed and brought into measure with the grace of free riming seeks to be embodied in the actuality of the work.   The initial sentences of the Confucian Analects—particularly the rays-wings ideogram—are kept in mind thruout, along with the role number has in the counted measures of Homer and of Zukofsky.   This vision goes back to my student correspondence with Ezra Pound and to an undergraduate general course in Confucius with the great Sinologist Peter Boodberg at the University of California in Berkeley over thirty years ago.

TWO SETS OF TENS: Derived from Confucian Analects

"Heaven is going to use your master as a bell with its wooden tongue"

"the understanding of all excellence and" Our standing would strive
"read chantingly" —divine the root right— "bring back the good"
of origins delight teaches word
exercise deeds exemplify will's intentions ply spirit rays ideogram our
commonality.   Learn dark to light bird flight wing fire air
earth lover song intending lore increase long nurture and benefit
in each night and day work, that place and time
work in us universe to stir conscience.
Pleasure is entire in perseverence and application. Heart's virtue rejoices
in company.   Ten years again to strive awakes mind's magic.

At once terse, liberal in energies, radical in effort, truth-
centerd, the second decade must contend
—willful stupefaction at large grows dangerous—military cliques and cartels
play into the hands of mean and fanatical men— swells

ambition. Note: midst what ever lies, ring true the way
remains ours to find, fierce to hold to, hard to bear
flight constantly live addresst to realize life's good uses
produces its own ease.   The fire increases and burns pure.
Ours the war against false leads—brightning mind
lifts soul in to its arms let love but regulate.

Robert Duncan/San Francisco
October 8, 1981

❖❖❖❖❖❖❖❖❖❖❖❖❖

THE REGULATORS   Set of Passages

THE DIGNITIES   [Passages]

Bonitas . Magnitudo . Eternitas . Potestas . Sapientia . Voluntas . Virtus . Veritas . Gloria

Blesst the black Night that hides the elemental germ,
the Day that brings the matter to light and its full term.
For goodness' sake we'll snuff the candle out and turn again to dark,
for there the spark occluded rests most firm   bright flower of what we know,   *bonny fleur,*
your seed returns to work in what we cannot know.

The smallest particle vertiginous exceeds the Mind.

But there is no act that is not chaind in its joy, Comedian, to the suffering of the world!
  this the Magnitudo   *this*   the gaze clear into the depths of the grandeur.
    Hel   in its coals winking   the sound of a moan I hear in the music
        song comes from   in the radiant adoration   design's heart

      here   my devotion   in the overwhelming   ever immediate, ever remote.

The numbers belong to a set addresst to Eternity   the uncountable.

  "The zero stands without a sound   *unaussprechlich*
  "Round and formd just like an O   *recht wie ein O*

  Die Rechenbücher among the first popular didactic works to be printed"—
    Poetry must go back to whose orders.

Numeration   Addition   Subtraction   Duplation   Mediation   Miltiplication   Division   Reduction

where thruout there is *Elevation*   the grouping of units into smaller numbers of higher units
and *Resolution*   the de-grouping of higher units into lower ones.

  There is truly no direction   no "center" to the "center"   our sounding
    goes out as we go out   no circumference to the "circumference"

          perilous then   time and space   as we reckon

    we but follow a beckoning   in measure   haunted

  "without actually performing any true computation at all"

The Power holds   in what we do   undoing   claim.

    And of Hipparchus   lost in the Sea   (we have to do with imaginary numbers and John Keats)

        where we are   here   outside What Is.

    But here we speak of the power of the Word, of the   fearful exchange we make.
    The numbers count   the line advances   music we hear that Music
        the Universe bestirs in us   enhances speech   *"So that"*

    we take time in writing   feet in our measures dance and   rime sounds harmonies

      setting up a *demeure*   "in uncertainties, mysteries, doubts"
       something there we "hear"   hearing imitates   the poem *itself*   our abode

        becomes Intention   to its Law   abiding.

Acknowledged in each part   moving immediate   in-dwelling   song comes from   co-operate
  the whole proposes itself in assorted keys   to wander   yet   in each step
instrumental   drawing breath and releasing breath   takes place

    in passage belonging to a design in passage   drawing the sort   for ratio.

Wisdom as such must wonder   for sortilege   is all.   Thruout
    the magic-loving tongue speaks and tastes

      thunder   the radiance of the sun upon the leaf.

And among the poet's chimeras of an afternoon   the moth's
    ephemeral existence   take key in mystery
      translates. . . . what?   The event   courses direct

        comes "from"?

To volunteer   *ite, missa est*   my life when's done the feast I offer you   plunder
    my excess   but what's sweet and true I've meant to be the office
        the vowels in sequence   rime's offering
    the trumpet voluntary imitates the soul's release   Will's   not forced
nor reaches but   upon the ayre's promise   frees itself.   Entirely
    what we see, taste, hear, balance and   let go from balancing, hear to pace, feel
      the presence of   its scent   the fearful transport in every sense we know
    is given   we come to ourselves wherein   as if

      recovering,

born by the Virtue of this thing   —"God" will not suffice —*"My Lord"*'s but   a personal obedience
    I give them up   the savor of the Host was all   if it be not my condition
    and I at its disposal   liberal, radical, pluralistic, multiphasic my mind   most
        a part   not whole   nowhere total, no "where" to be fulfilld—
    the *Virtu* of What Is is propositional   realms within realms   secreted
        "seem".   "He", "She"   are mysteries for Love I've drawn upon
    the Dignities exceed.   The Good remains.   I cannot dispose of it—
        the good of living, the good of aging, the good of the alchemical changes
            I love in loving
                    —"God"'s but Mind's hint at the Sublime
            I'd not think to surpass

Veritas.   In truth, Beauty   is a ninth Dignity   hidden in the   fitness.

    In a flash   the Lie   seen   truly what it is   —drive thru to the very core—
            to err   is to   find out   anew   this What   we know   persists
        fitful tho it comes to us   in starts   whose spectral presence underlies
                —it is the ground of us—
            every "where" presides   —follow the leader and its music rides as we go.

    True to what is happening   having no "own self" but   faithful as an arrow here intention hides

        finds its target in each   coming to

GLORIA   into color   flare   vermilion petal o'er pale green leaf   blue star and violet
    deep purple into bronze   wing spread   into golden wing   bright yellow spoil
    Spring's prolific patterning   and here, a further shade within the shade
    the eye draws in   where trembling leaf by leaf among a slumbering mass   light
        strikes   its momentary elections   the passage or *limen*   the where-Glory-abounds
    all around   mounting   the blare into the resounding brass   the "distant" trumpeting
        all the concert of strings beneath the soaring bows   now thundering "Now"
        drawn into a shimmering one tone   and in this universe a vast attending
    glorious uprising   clash on clash of a great noise   roar out-of-bounds abounding
        praise on praise   in every instrument of life   Hosannah loud and deep   unto the heights

lovely,   all, alone   wavering   courageous   venturing melody   light   an ayre upon the air

rising   falling   turning returning   taking hold   its beautiful secret in a heart-beat breathing

    (the orchestral tumult, the announcement and summa   remains thruout) yet clear-cut   true-toned   resolute   the extending scale of an imagined humanity its home

having no place in "fact"

abiding

there is this last voice, first voice   this "Gloria"   this one beginning

flower of song

this lingering of a scent in every thing.

THE FIRST   [Passages]

the one ground   of Learning   a life

to live

—the Word Itself   has no other

foundation.

To lie   eats at the life-root.   Truth

has its force   not in itself virtue   but in the intensification

the individual life finds.

The eye that avoids seeing   sickens.

Speech has only the one heart immediate to come from

—this   the preaching for the day,

in each one living   the one tongue

Yet in the imagination   potential the world!

so that there is no ancient wisdom except in each   the ancient —from the initial
thrust of the elements in evolution living in their momentary adventure alone—

life of the universe appointed.

60

IN THIS MUSIC   (Webern):   *"Every thing is a principal idea."*
                          Every where central to enquiry.

        Every time initial.

The people of this nation thruout time are not one but a multitude   each from his one
            heart/mind   coming forward   masst

so you cannot strike down our leader   for no *one*   leads us—

        you will be exhausted before *we* are to strike down the

                multitude of volitions we come from.   "War"

        you have set as the first   priority   —the most   profitable
            in a system of wasting the world—

                                    Locate where I am   where I come from

—it is a lonely place   —no other   —do you find me out?

        This nation of a people   each separate from each
                        listening   calling   hearing   recalling

this adventuring of a soul   the aloneness in Truth Love must come from   go toward—

    yet a cry repeated by a thousand sentinels,
    an order relayd by a thousand bearers of rumor   where

mutualities awaken,   string upon string   vibrates   its own meaning of "War"   shakes
        more than you bargaind for.

                        "I too   also sing War"

Whitman answers the Muse of History, of the state with its armies and of the would be makers of revolutions

    "and a longer and greater one than any"—   As in 1937

    I thought Trotsky might mean by his slogan of the Permanent Revolution   such a life
            perennial   breaking forth from all we knew of life

        declaration in the midst of all orders, dictatorships of madness or of reason,

            from all reasons, from projects for the future   deeper identities

                states of emergency

        of the PRIMARY   the unforeseen   the Eros-Need.

"for the Body and for the Eternal Soul
Lo, I too am come,   chanting the chant of battles"

in Hunger   this Dignity   Sapientia   —it is indeed a fire—

Van Gogh's making for us to see   the soul-truth of this peach tree in bloom   speech

burst forth into flamboyant meaning   —it is the ensemble of colors the painting brings forth

leaf tongues—

no argument   yet to see

ces malédictions,   ces blasphèmes,   ces plaintes   the tree beyond its nature burgeoning

ces extases,   ces cris—

a call of lost hungers in the great forest   the Truth of Nature beyond our nature   it goes

wherever the passionate   Life grows in our life   and the blood flows.

STIMMUNG   [Passages]

the outpourings of personal love   the magic names   the true intonation
"and after these have become false they must constantly be found again"

and after these have become lost   the truth of the false there is   must be constantly found out

'transformations' – 'varied deviations' – 'pulsations' = 'assimilations'   —is it all so composed?

yet constant.

So the Preacher arises again   just when, exalted, we would call upon the Dignities
and   luminous   self-evident   transcendent   these, governing, take their stand

HE takes over the voice   raising his tone, exhorts,   aborts just temperament—
the Canticle of the sublime regents yields to his cant

And from the beginning of Time

I have brought down from the mountain this mighty presumption I put on

    the mask of righteousness   the Law-Giver   the fire of wrath   this megaphone

    me the stony Zoroaster speaks again.

The Master Architect has arranged horizons in a renewing design.

At the end of the avenue of golden trees   —no, they are funereal and black—
    the illusion of a vanishing point contradicts the judgment of the eye

    and what was far is suddenly here   —in every phrase change the phases of color—

    the bright array of tulips,   ranunculi,   rare hyacinthus
        the very death-bloom-phalloi   not the flowers you know by that name
        but the spreading pallor of a lavender-and-gold   answering tears of the lost boy—

    a circle of alabaster columns   ceremonial   stairs ascend   the garden enclose opens

"Here I have released the bounds of my allotted space.   Here I shape   the opening of the Mind Field"

            The Two Sides address each other

     As if from the limits of Art there were this breathless allowance,   this rest
        before Vertigo.   An address to the Timeless.

—Excoriating the exploitation of Earth and the deceit of palatial designs

     the Master of the Reality Principle harangues the passersby   *—Turn from your Pleasures!*

        You, enthralld by the turnings of the lyre's music!

    shake from your nerves' ends the leading thrill of this poet's dream—

the outpourings of personal love

                —the Golden Vanity sails in this song"

    all night long the magic names   *daimones*   entering and leaving bodies   in thrall

    the genius of the five-fingered hand   moving the arm,   the wand   conducting the mind in time

        the enraptured Hyacinth in the Death Game   Him-the-God-Loved

           deep purple   fathomless

But I am the Mouth of the Wretched   howling   I am loud-speaker of the Injured.

I have taken offense unto dying   at the thriving of this system of vigorous mediocrity.

I rant against the rulers.   I am come from the ranks of jealous men.   To ruin the illusions of music

the knife of injustice has been driven home in me.

Nothing is lovely in the End of this Time!

All the Time   the Nine actors   stand   "motionless"   staring   into the

Mind-Space-Time project   the "depth" our perspectives seek out   hearing

in the grace of a new music   the root the Preacher thinks to come from

very like the aura of this Falling-in-Love   Stimmung.

Do they countenance the grinding down of lives,   the
poisons pouring out from fortunes and powers,   Here sound their "A"?

Do they overlook   this ruining of the ways?

As if their faces were flowers   the immoveable masks of the Dignities

open to the air   lure and regard of a persisting world

Aussi   —passage de Baudelaire encore—
où la Fatuité promène son extase   *vois ce souris fin et voluptueux*

(as Whalen years ago addresst me   —*dear fatuous Duncan*)

in verliebten Tagen   ("love-bitten" the translation on the record jacket has it)

bei San Francisco   und am Meerufer   der vieldeutig ist   die REINE Stimmung

(in welches Wort "stekt 'Stimme'"   Obertöne zum Grundton

the preaching in earnest, over-ernest   the Love-claim into avowal   seeks ear nest

the almost accusing   SPEECH   strange bird-song

flowers

[Stockhausen]   von Atmosphäre   von Fluidum   von *seelischen* gestimmheit

drawn

in impermanent lines.

ENTHRALLD   [Passages]

by myth, story patternings   wish full, dread full   of last things

anciently "ours"   lasting   what else the thrall

but this lasting

this place   this hour   –   by resonances   notes of Who "I" is   sounded

thruout we search   to be   "He", "She", and "It"   three persons in the presentation move

where you and I   willing to be entranced and

in the enhancement wary   read   into the third person

pass   ourselves   lost

as if in speaking begun the world at last would complete itself in "us"

and we become there parts of speech   "told"

confer Wittgenstein: "How did we learn 'I dreamt so and so'?"

"When you see trees swaying about they are talking to one another"

about what   I do not know   I read into the sway

I cannot see the wind   but the light shimmering in the leaves dances in the wind's confusion to speak

I hear in seeing

Still   the flesh sings
fresh from making love   our two bodies
stretcht upon each other   tuning
turning and returning   beyond
eucalyptus trees in one foliage dance with the wind in their branches
and your eyes shine   answering
the deep going shine and tone I have been
      released into.
How young my sixty-one years are in me!
How just arrived where I am again I can be.
It is just this afternoon   just this hour
yet how entirely life races
in the blue of the sky my eyes find themselves
      feeding sight

as in the arousal of your body thriving
the long embrace, repeated mouthings
the mounting thrill in one shared trunk,
                one spirit shining,
filld with the sense of you
still the flesh sings . . .

"I might choose between calling a melody

'lovely' and calling it 'youthful'"

. . . "'Spring Symphony'"

QUAND LE GRAND FOYER DESCEND DANS LES EAUX   [Passages]

"His attempted suicide   seemd
        to purge his nature of depression and despair"

        having to do with spelling, with error, with words . . .

La scène monte et. . .   what is today's beauty?
        this wetting of the world   tearful
and into leaf-flame flares   —rocks, trees—
        mélange de principes   dreams also of this order
        letting go   into a lovely litter
elle s'épanouit en tons mélangés
                Narcissus alone   comes   to see
                        les arbres,   les rochers

        his face destitute in beauty

les granits se mirent dans les eaux . . .
        based on other functions   a music still
                water means to reflect
rain   drops interrupt the mirror   . . . *y déposent*
        bare in winter   cold face   in summer clothed
leurs reflets
                        into shadow close

the poem mounts toward a stem in time

    staring down into its foliage

the sap rises to see
       it's Death lingering   mine
    (returning to Baudelaire)
       he is staring down into his book

looking at what he has written   just now

   the entire passage has to do with color

     the thought of suicide before

takes on light and shade near and far a

   way.   The eye

dwells on the horizon.

IN BLOOD'S DOMAINE   [Passages]

The Angel Syphilis in the circle of Signators   looses its hosts   to swarm
   mounting the stem of being   to the head
                       Baudelaire, Nietszche, Swift
   are not cased into Death
              the undoing of Mind's rule in the brain.
  "Yet it is in spirit that nature is timelessly enveloped."   And, as above, so below
                                there are
    spirochete invasions that eat at the sublime envelope,   not alien, but familiars
    Life in the dis-ease radiates   invisibilities devour my star

and Time restless crawls in center upon center   cells of lives within life conspire
  Hel shines in the very word *Health*   as *Ill* in the Divine Will shines.
    The Angel Cancer crawls across the signs of the Zodiac to reach its
appointed time   and   bringing down the carnal pride   bursts into flower—

Swift, Baudelaire, Nietszche   into the heart Eternal of what Poetry is

      answer to the genius and science of the Abyss.   The first sign of this
                                      advancing power

shows in Fear that goes   clear to the bone   to gnaw at the marrow.

The seeress Lou Andreas-Salomé   sees long before the hour arrives—

    [mais] *"Tantôt sonnera l'heure   où le divin Hasard,*

où l'auguste Vertu, ton épouse encore vierge"   —where black the infected blood

    gushes forth from Rilke's mouth, from his nose, from his rectal canal

      news his whole body bears as its truth   of the septic rose

Où le Repentir même   (oh!   *la dernière auberge!*)

                      Lovely then

that Death come to carry you away from the moment of this splendor
    that bursts the cells of your body   like a million larvæ triumphant

    comes to life in the fruit   All the spreading seeds,   the viral array
    taking over flesh as the earth it is

                scarlet eruptions

And the pneumatics torn in the secret workings of the Angel Tuberculosis

(No, I do not speak of Evils or of Agents of Death   but these Angels
    are attendants of lives raging within life,   under these Wings we dread

viruses, bacilli   come home to thrive in us   où tout te dira

    "Meurs, vieux lâche!   il est trop tard!"   Die, you old coward,
      it is too late.   I feel the ringing of tomorrow's bell.

But what ate at Pound's immortal Mind?   for the Cantos,   for *Les Fleurs du Mal*
    so eat at Mind's conscience
    what malady?   what undoing-of-all-Good   workt behind speech?

    —are the matter I come from—these poisons I must know the hidden intentions of
    where "this coil of Geryon" (Djerion) said Mr Carlyle,   who now becomes

    Thomas Carlyle, not the member of Congress, but
             the genius of "Hero Worship"   his (our) congress

And if I know not my wound   it does not appear to suppurate?   In this intercourse
   "Adolf furious from perception"   —does this thought refer to Hitler?

   Link by link I can disown no link of this chain from my conscience.

      Would you forget the furnaces of burning meat   purity demands?
      There is no ecstasy of Beauty in which I will not remember Man's misery.

   Jesus, in this passage   —He is like a man coming forward in a hospital theater—
      cries out: I come not to heal but to tear the scab from the wound you wanted
                                                                           to forget.
      May the grass no longer spread out to cover the works of man in the ruin of
                                                                           earth.

   What Angel,   what Gift of the Poem,   has brought into my body

         this sickness of living?   Into the very Gloria of Life's theme and variations
            my own counterpart of Baudelaire's terrible Ennuie?

AFTER PASSAGE   [Passages]

      And if terror be the threshold of Angelic In-Formation,   the Masters
of Nuclear Power, malevolent dreamers,   knowing and unknowing
      (Einstein before Roosevelt urging the project of the Bomb to defeat Hitler)
      undo the inner structure at the atomic level to release its energies

out from millions upon millions of suns   the Angel of this Polluting radiance
      streams,   does and undoes the concordances of the DNA helix,   viral fragments

   Mind comes into this language as if into an Abyss.

   The Scenario: the fear of fascism that brought the dedicated group of Los Alamos
      the hope, after V.E.Day, that the bomb wouldn't be needed after all;
      the pleas that the bomb's aweful power ought to be shown to the world before it is used;

("Nothing" is happening in these words in their accumulating sentence but the
            mounting delusions of a compulsive psychosis)

Hitler defeated   yet they continue to work to realize the Bomb   sleep-workers
    the marvelous Toy   the despair after Hiroshima

The other face of the Angel, not now   of War but of Peace-Time uses—
    from the promised power stations   radioactive waste   death-leakings

    come into the hour glass.

                     "The wall faced
a closed window, and the light flash from the
blast cast shadows upon the window frames that
imprinted themselves permanently on the wall"
"And the angle of these shadows allowed us to
prove that the bomb really did go off at exactly
the right altitude/"

In the poem   "light" and "right"   riming with "time" and   far back
                    —do you remember?—
    with "Mind" and the hidden   address to "Night" -

"shadows" and "windows"   where in this   "flash"   the "frames"
    indelibly imprint themselves—

                          shades and winds establisht   all
    where the angle allowd   or   proved
                            exactly the right passage—

I am but reading the signs.   The Signators enter my design.

    Whose boundaries?   In the Seal of this Angel

what spells   this scene that flows through and through us   these shadows

    exact   what Name?   hieroglyph of what Wish?

The Wind blows back from the corners of the Sea.

The lovely singer who again sends his message to the world from the elm tree
                is innocent of the holocaust.

Will I outlive the end of the rime I meant to come to?

Quiet, my soul, O   follow the lead of the Nuttall song sparrow.

    What is complete but rests in the momentary illusion.

WITH IN   [Passages]

strict form

alarms

bound to

and / or

charm love's

center

out side

work thru

him / her

undo

knots yes

in form

  ties

releasing

me to you

    A

   music

  at rest.

SEAMS   [Passages]

                                    eternal   wish
        the scenes dissolve

                        not into a fading of the light   the window
        focuses all in a higher resolution

                                        becomes this Mind
                each   flower and leaf
            in me   autumnal   day   and equinox
                    the coriander is in seed   swelling   a ruddy light in the green
        Sight   gathers   your radiant   smile   and the ripening smell
            into natural crowns the sun and wind address their declarations.

            When will be the Harvest of this Wheat?

            Eternal   It is harvested   in Time.
                                                Reap
                    what treasure from life's stemming tide
                at each tip   the stop   where   growth fills   burns dry

                        gathering   but to   scatter   the brown resolve
        falls   the words seem to fall into measures of the song   to rise
                as if this movement of the air   essential sememes of the voice   bear

        and every I   awake in me   —This dark is morning?—
                the call   -   the work   -   the Now   I hearkens to

YOU, Muses,   [Passages]

                              Ἔσπετε νῦν μοι

Tell me now   ὑμεῖς γὰρ θεαί 'ἐστε, πάρεστέ τε   facing forever What Is   immediate

          ἰστέ τε πάντα   hidden women   who make up and unmake   "my" mind   All

discover in me my dwelling in earth-hold and air   in this time

      and place "insteede of laborious and sober enquirie

      of truth"   "hopes and beliefes"   as such   become "strange and impossible shapes"

      The sybil alone   sees there   oracular forms   οὐκ ἂν ἐγὼ μυθήσομαι οὐδ ὀνομήνω

Mnemosyne above directing   remind me, attendant Muses   μνησαίαδ' ὅσοι

      αὐ . . . ἐρέω
      ἡμεῖς δὲ κλέος οἶον ἀκούομεν οὐδέ τι ἴδμεν   our having

                  no more than truth's rumors and our learning no knowing is

      broken themes in passages of the wind heard

      Erato   here   Muse of the Kithara, sing for me   sing me   blowing

                  upon that reed

          yet the charge of a note coming into our histories   that allure   touching

                  songs rise and fall   enchanting   what government regulates

          this state of Mind   the beat steady   where we wonder.

                        ❖❖❖❖❖❖❖❖❖❖❖❖❖❖

73

STRUCTURE OF RIME: OF THE FIVE SONGS

Not having found *The Five Songs*, a sound and then an other is sent out to search meaning.   But *The Five Songs* is not hidden there.   In the sounding alone there is a rumor of *The Five Songs*.   They, the Five, are earth, air, fire, and water, and an other.   They are four suites—hearts, diamonds, clubs, spades, and another.   Spring, summer, fall, winter—four seasons and one other.   They are the five vowel-letters and each one is an other.

Are there five songs in *The Five Songs* or is *The Five Songs* a book of the Five?   Up, down, strange, and charm, written in sets of flavor and color.   But "flavor" and "color" here are not what we mean by flavor and color.   There are at least five such excited states.   The search for the fifth element, for naked beauty, as it is calld, has proved much more difficult than the search for naked charm was.   There are five points in the rime.

A note in the course of the structures of rime where no rime was certain the nature of our time is hidden in the rime of *The Five Songs*.

THE FIVE SONGS

*

Do you come from my heart,
sweet penetrating drum?

Do you breathe upon reeds of the stars,
far reaching melody where Love
seeks ever still to arrive lingering
notes and rests you need?

No, Beloved Sleeper, the beat you hear
repeats in the awakening of all hearts
the seed of a fire in the heart of What Is.

What Is enters and seeks to arouse you
     from sleep
to this dance day calls for
     night works.

Yes, from your heart it is I
        speaking,   the Lord of the Stars.
My never-to-be-completed seeking
        completion is the music
that reaches out to you so
        stirring this reaching in you.

Now your body moves from the hub.
Your mind turns out
        from the divine spring
        in bridal clothes.

The reed and the head of the drum
                                /
                                    call for this

immediate answering call
        and recall
the bow upon its string sounds.

                        *

In the five songs the five fingers
        of my right hand seek out
        the eternal   governing

song hidden from me I
        have from the beginning loved.

The five fingers of my left hand
        keep a count they tell
        of this Tale of this Lover
                and the Beloved.

My right hand enters Night to
        undo the fastenings of your
        clothes,
My left hand knows its way
        to your nipples
        and goes there

where the long promised ayre this
        is the instrument of
floods thru me as I
        flood thru you —   Who is this

figure ever unlockt in the play
    of the keys?

        In the five songs
there are four songs that are
    the work of my life,
all that life coming from and
    returning to five.

This bell tolls the hours in
    the spell of the Tale that will
    never be told, the Unending

ever in the unfolding

This bell liquid and clear
    sounds the undoing
of what is bound, the opening
    in the ways.

        These keys

    commingling
            left and right

my fingers lose self
    in the configuration this music
    unlocks in me.

        *

My sister opens a window in order
    to see   where I am
the wind out there   comes in here
    to sing in the order of the song

there is a soughing, a rushing
    thru the meshes as the theme
    weaves,   a rustling
of leaves of the book as I read

the Sea comes into it, into
    this turning of pages,

this Song of Reiterations
    combing over littoral
boundaries,   mounting,
    retracting,   there is
the third poem given over to Law,
the fourth poem   to War,

     and before
the first poem   this
  moaning at the barriers
the ear in the depths of the shell hears

   the lion-roar not of fire
     but of water

this   so far away   or is it
    long ago   sound of the Beast
upon the shore of the Beast
    we sleep by.

My sister searches the night sky,
    its swarm upon swarm of stars,
    and calls for me.

I answering
  how still it is out there where
  she sees me— stand

in her recall   my song

this Song of Retributions
the Will advancing Law upon
    Law   withdrawing,

devouring the time where I am,
undoing and restoring itself

Song of Eternal Restitutions
and the Refusal at work therein

goes out to reach her

needing it   whose true voice

    a flame guttering in a high wind

*

Having you in mind I was where I
among the shadows of Saint John of Persia   am

in a Time of Wars seeking the end of Time
the Song of What War shall I sing?
would-be shaman of no tribe I know.

How hard it was then to say.
Yet it was a song of coming to you
    where you were not,
a song of longing where you were to be.

You and I are not "we" but
each in each other's light and shadow
    commingling   the years
gathering what we alone may mean.

If in the sham of a rhetoric
the "kingdom" were restored, and the king
of that story should come forth from his shadow
calling for the heroic in us,

On what side will the Good be?
On what side the Evil?   I am foreign
to this country where I find myself.
The five senses err in me.

And it will be the same as before.
The line of the song follows an errant course.
Only the romance of being true,
nonsense alone our faith holds to.   Still,

the moon remains,
the desire of the earth after rain within me.

Let the vanity of mere writing go.
Was I carried away?   by a vanity?

But we have been waiting
—how deep day's phantasy or nightmare
        has yet to go—
the day slips from us,
the levels of water fall.
The light falls, revealing a canyon.

Even in dreams I am what I have
        thought myself to be.

                        *

What is "Sea" the name of?   What is
      "Wind"?   What "heart"?   What "fire"?

The illusive finds us out.
The unnameable draws from us a world
        of names.

Invisible, the light is reflected by
        every thing.
What we took to be the horizon, elusive,
        everywhere touches,   familiar,
        too familiar.

Estranged, the moon
shines in the depths of a restless sea.
Five notes of this scale answer
        five stars as if
among these millions there were
        the sign of what is eternal.

Yet I had only this one song to sing
in the five.   This bell
        sounding this one hour
        my life is   this single note
        in me belonging
to configurations of this   ascension

              wind rose in the air   even as
below   descending

        goes deep to   sound underground.

What does "you" mean where the thought
        of you accompanies and leads me

the grace of note after note

                              we are

almost there   but O,   Dear
        as I sang then

        I have always been   here

where you were   I sound my refrain the "Sea"
        releases,   the "heart"
            in the earliest poem awaited,

        Again I have arrived.

         "Wind" and "Fire"
        take up the signature

        beyond   naming.

                                   April 5–27, 1981

                        *

WHOSE   [Passages]

[for Jim Hillman's
tribute to Henri Corbin
The Thought of the Heart

                    Hot blood, cold blood

the "I" came to the doctor   not the psyche-anal-ist

                              but that specter

     of the Heart
            —me cowerd in the corner

        take care – κῆρ – κῆρ

the etymology is false   but   where else but the
    heart does this   cold   sit?

"The throat" the poet declares   "knows the stop:

     A door opens in self   dry grief, shame, guilt it is

             door-man   double-hinge

             blood/air pump   ex-

change artist   here to trust   adventure's

    order.   Sing if you want to   but hear me,

      coy sparrow,   in truth troth

      you gotta go   ready to lose all—

"I" came to be cured of   "me" in his wrong place,

    her fancy-full   myriad minded   rain-beau or rein-bow

no trister-god —trickster that is— but trickt out

           dog in the downpour

—a door   you're not to believe
in the twister came   my

self pretender   might have   not been there

but my heart was in my throat   I could not   not *know*   my blood

pressure crested as if to arrest

I will name many times this uprising
—political, mental, sexual, social   —you name it—   mounting rung by rung

this climax   to what overview

under the double-axe

Life in the storm-cloud hides

in this persona   thunder to sound
strike from the text this   inflatus/deflatus

big wind mouth

the fierce sparrow nests down meek in the cold of the blast

the tiger seeks shelter from his element of fire

Who then sings this
sweet song?   Who then roars?

Who then   is this passion

that returns for me?   who then
that remembers and goes back for me?

"I" – "me"   no longer mine   —your

sudden call   I did not mean

to climb the ladder of

Feb. 19, 1982

CLOSE

             At the brim,   at the lip

       the water   the word   trembles   fills

          to flooding   every thing

       (Olson's "elements in trance")   advancing

       this river   deeper than Jordan   flows

everywhere   the spirit bird/fish   comes down into the medium

    comes up into the medium   lighter than Jordan

          the Grail-Heart holds   this Mystery

    does not fill in time   but through out time   fills

    —dove-sound,   sparrow-song,   whippoorwill-cry—

    —salmon-swirl,   trout stream,   gold carp in the shadow pool—

Wish   the daimon of this field   force
                force before the gods came.

All the rest is archetype: Plato's in the Mind
    or Jung's   in psyche,   yes,   glorious

             imaginal   But this clime

is Fancy's   that something beyond the given
    come into it   that
    this rare   threatend—   I too want to
    prove it out
                    imaginary Love

I do not "really" feel   I live by.

So it is not the Holy Ghost,
I do not have the Ghost of a Chance in it,

          still,   at the brim,   at the lip

What else trembling   but this pretend
    pretentious   pre-text   Child's play of answering

where   what was not calld for

this too   this playing-house   hold

—You think I have some defense for it,   in it?
      do not know the critical impossibility?

I make my realm this realm in the
            patently irreal—   History
      will disprove my existence.

The Book will not hold this poetry   yet
      all the vain song I've sung comes into it

                  spirit-bird cuckoo's   Song of Songs

one tear of vexation as if it were beautiful

                  falls into the elixir

            one tear of infatuation follows
                  as if it were love

Let something we must all wonder about   ensue

            one tear I cannot account for   fall

this: the flooding into the flooding

this: the gleam of the bowl in its not holding—

                              Feb. 19, 1982

AT THE DOOR

Elegbara   open the Way   Fate ruling   All   out going   the Flooding beyond
     Powers of ancient Africa, come forward   into the Rage of the Nation

     Humanity dies out, the heart hardens   that has denied you—

     What is "Race" when Changes of Messages
               mark Life as His Passage?

The approaches of Spring   The lily towers   unfurling abroad leaf and white flower

     And You   who turn Fate like a key   in the lock Fate is   attend

     the passage of Time in its trammels   the passage of Soul   unfold

     But in what "Africa"?   gave myself   entirely over to this   Confidence-Man,
          Trickster,   deep going Forger of Story   Master to   pretend-me.

At the downrushing of the Spring   unbound from Reason.

     I am Child of the Abyss.   Legba,   what then does the color of my skin sign?
     What Seal in the flesh leaves this   Falls   into something beyond   opens in me?

          The tongue will talk in my mouth. Wild words enter as you will this stream—
     Let me give me up to his   use of me. "Each of us,"   my sister said . . .

          At the mouth of the Dee   my grandfather the Story-Teller
          flows into World-Dream   our ancestor   papa loa divino

"belongs to a series of stories"   —Janvier, Mars, Mai, Juillet, Août, Octobre have *bon âme*—
in the dark of the personal shadow   *gros-bon-ange*   shines   *(p) ti-bon-ange* in penumbra
     —December dangerous—
                         . . . "which ones do you belong to?"

               In this Story calld Now   hear I make *ma demeure*

     l'uvri bayè pu mwê   Papa-Legba   l'uvri bayè

     pu mwe pasé   Maît'bitasyon   Let me past.

          Pass on.   In the passage beyond   faire mon habitation

          I pass out in reading   divine the text   intoxicate

               mine to divine.

ILLUSTRATIVE LINES

i

This pen is where the writing flows in sight
the measuring eye follows line by line,
mouth set in the mind's movement throughout at-
tentive, tentative —let the numbers fall
into the hands   one drawing the letters   one
by one   holds the count at bay,   the other
keeps the time of an inner wave in sway.

All is enfolded in a body of thought
the body occupies.   The taut brow bends over
this work in words   studious as a lover
caught up on this telling of a tale the ear
attends the wary listening of,   as if to hear
as that reader   entirely his   other
hears the ring of truth in the sound of it
the writing is mute witness to.

ii

The eye now follows mute witness to the text
the mouthing delites to analyze
and the hand directs the mind to music—

all intellect is in this fingering of time advanced
that knows no horizon of learning—
the reaches of this aptitude for exacting measure's
    due   the heart
waits upon   the breath flows from—

whose then the resident identity?   Voice
is all.   How accurately the portraitist must draw
the instrumental skull, delineate the ear, to make
a speaking likeness,   for sound
    is what   everywhere
        draws near.

The body at work exemplifies the work
back of whose eyes sight surfaces lives
beyond this life rush.   The forehead
leads forward against its dark wave.

What works in me is not mine but
ancient survivals,   how much withheld
strives unspeakable in the word to speak
the lips refuse,   eyes
close upon to face what Man is in this.

Child, not of Our Father, but of the Abyss
where He was.   In the fires of that mine
Love comes to Grief to strike a light
again,   and Dark increases to enhance
the pathos of a brief humanity time allows
              not easily.

iv

Still the face reflects a pool of thought
having nor subject nor object
resolute in tranquility   deep the eyes
gaze into the myriad nights and days
space that is time, time that is space
beyond horizon,   nor is there a center to this Mind—
it's as if all the visible were Invisible,
identical with the blue presence of the nenuphar.

v

And lust into the luster of that glow   resolves
in memory   this depth is lustral and
      melody grows in me   dim
frequencies of that water-lily head
the hands in keeping time   address

                              to illustrate

this   almost unmoving bliss in movement
                lustrum upon lustrum float
shadowy petalld fingerd five upon five
          the right hand and the left hand
in feeling   lift the mind upon the air
              passing over the water

in this   dance beyond consciousness   leading
                    —an other
unheard beat its eternal governance—
              sight and sound
pass into the transports of a lingering

              scent

              illustrious.

AFTER A LONG ILLNESS

No faculty not   ill at ease
      lets us
      begin where I must

from the failure of systems   breath
      less,   heart
      and lungs water-logd.

Cloggd with light chains   the kidneys'
      condition is terminal   life

the light and the heavy, the light
      and dark.   It has always been
close upon a particular Death, un
      disclosed   what's behind

seeing, feeling, tasting, smelling   —that Cloud!

For two years
bitterness pervaded:

in the physical body   the high   blood pressure
      the accumulation of toxins, the
      break-down of ratios,

in the psyche "stewd in its own juices"
      the eruption of hatreds, the prayer
—I didn't have a prayer—   your care
      alone kept my love clear.

I will be there again   the ways
      must become crosst   and again
      dark passages,   dangerous straits.

My Death attended me and I knew
      I was not going to die,
nursed me thru.   Life took hold.

What I ate   I threw up
and crawld thru as if turnd inside out.
      Every thought I had I saw
sickend me.   Secretly
      in the dark   the filters
      of my kidneys   petrified   and my Death
rearranged the date He has with me.

*

Yes, I was afraid
of not seeing you again,   of being
      taken away, not
of dying, the specter I have long
      known as my Death is the
Lord of a Passage that unites us;
      but of
      never having come to you that other
specter of my actually living is.
      Adamant.

"I have given you a cat in the dark," the voice said.
Everything changed in what has always been there
at work in the Ground: the two titles
      "Before the War",   and now, "In the Dark"
underwrite the grand design.   The magic
      has always been there,   the magnetic purr
      run over me, the feel as of cat's fur
charging the refusal to feel.   That black stone,
      now I see, has its electric familiar.

In the real I have always known myself
      in this realm where no Wind   stirs
      no Night
turns in turn to Day,   the Pool of the motionless water,
      the absolute Stillness.   In the World, death after death.
In this realm,   no last thrall of Life stirs.
      The imagination alone knows this condition.
As if this were before the War,   before
      What Is,   in the dark this state
that knows nor sleep nor waking, nor dream
      —an eternal arrest.